**When Maya heard that Mr. Freeman was dead,
she stopped speaking.**

She was terrified. She thought his death was her fault. She felt that she was terrible. She thought that if she spoke to other people, they might die, too.

No one could reach her except Bailey. Her silence made the Baxters angry. They wanted her to play and laugh. Finally, Maya and Bailey were put on a train and sent back to Stamps.

Meet
Maya
ANGELOU

By Valerie Spain

Landmark Books®

Random House New York

Photo credits: AP/Wide World Photos, pages vi, 4, 37, 76, 79; The Billy Rose Theatre Collection, The New York Public Library for the Performing Arts, page 51; Dwight Carter, cover; Flip Schulke, page 62; Globe Photos, pages iii, 65; Magnum Photos, Inc., pages 9, 58; Martha Swope Photography, Inc./The Billy Rose Theatre Collection, The New York Public Library for the Performing Arts, page 67; Mary Ellen Mark/Library, pages 40, 73, 81, 85; Morgan & Marvin Smith/The Schomburg Center for Research in Black Culture, New York Public Library, page 47, Photofest, pages 11, 12, 13, 48, 82.

Excerpt from "Lift Ev'ry Voice and Sing" by James Weldon Johnson and J. Rosamond Johnson used with permission of Edward B. Marks Music Co.

www.randomhouse.com/kids

Library of Congress Cataloging-in-Publication Data
Spain, Valerie.
Meet Maya Angelou / by Valerie Spain.
p.   cm. — (Landmark books)
SUMMARY: A biography of the multifaceted African American woman Maya Angelou, tracing her life from her childhood in the segregated South to her prominence as a well-known writer.

ISBN 0-375-82465-0

1. Angelou, Maya—Juvenile literature. 2. Author, American—20th century—Biography— Juvenile literature. 3. Civil rights workers—Biography—Juvenile literature. 4. Entertainers—United States—Biography—Juvenile literature. 5. African American authors—Biography—Juvenile literature. [1. Angelou, Maya. 2. Authors, American. 3. African Americans—Biography. 4. Women—Biography.]
I. Title. PS3551.N464Z886 2003 818'.5409—dc21 2003043103

Printed in the United States of America 10 9 8 7 6 5 4 3 2 1
RANDOM HOUSE and colophon and LANDMARK BOOKS and colophon are registered trademarks of Random House, Inc.

Contents

Maya Angelou reading her poem
"On the Pulse of Morning."

I

On the Pulse of Morning

Maya Angelou looks up at the blue sky over the dome of the Capitol Building and smiles. She's not as nervous as she thought she'd be. In a few moments she will be reading a poem to the nation. It is Inauguration Day, January 20, 1993. Bill Clinton is about to take office as the forty-second president of the United States.

Maya received a phone call in November, shortly after Election Day. Bill Clinton had just won. A man who worked on the president's inaugural committee was on the line. He told her the new president-to-be wanted her to write a poem for his inauguration.

She later told a friend she was so "bowled over" that she had to sit down.

Then Maya got busy. She spent hours reading and writing and thinking. She used a pen and several pads of paper. She wrote and rewrote. The president's request would have been a great honor for any poet. But Maya Angelou was the first woman and the first African American to be so honored. Her poem *had* to be good. When she was finished, her poem was two pages long. She called it "On the Pulse of Morning."

Now she is in Washington, ready to read her poem to the president and the nation.

There is a platform raised above the crowd. Many important people are seated there.

Maya walks along the red carpet to the platform. People begin clapping. The tall black woman walks slowly and with great dignity. The new president is clapping harder than anyone.

From the platform Maya can see far down the lawn to the Washington Monument. Behind her sit the most powerful people in the country—the new president and vice president; former presidents; and the chief justice of the Supreme Court.

She waits for silence. Then she begins:

"A Rock, A River, A Tree..."

Maya Angelou's poem speaks for the Earth. It asks for peace. It asks Americans to face the past with courage and the future with hope. It speaks to people of all races

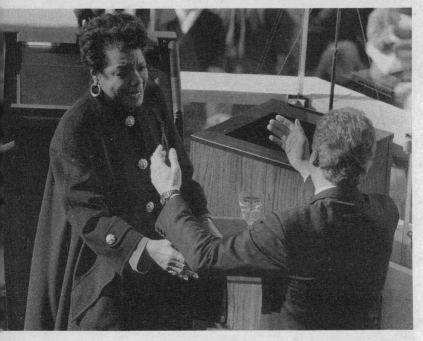

President Clinton approaches Maya for a hug.

and all nations. It asks them to face each
other and their country "on the pulse of this
new day."

As she finishes, the crowd cheers wildly.

President Clinton hugs her and says he loves her poem. He is going to frame it and hang it in the White House.

On that January day, at the age of sixty-four, Maya Angelou was at the peak of her career. She was famous and successful. But the road to Washington had not been easy. Not easy for a black child growing up poor in the farmlands of the American South. Maya Angelou stood before America and the world as a celebrated poet. She had come a long way from the poor and tiny town of Stamps, Arkansas.

2

A Place of Light and Shadow

The little girl sat looking out the train window. She pulled at a tag tied to her wrist. The tag said: "This is Marguerite Johnson, from Long Beach, California. She is going to Stamps, Arkansas. She will be picked up by Mrs. Annie Henderson."

The girl looked at her brother, Bailey. He was four years old—only one year older than she was. It was the year 1931. Their parents' unhappy marriage had ended. They had divorced. Daddy was sending them to his mother in Arkansas. He did not go with them. They were traveling hundreds of miles alone. Often other black people took care of them.

Right now a black woman sat next to Bailey. She had one arm around his shoulders, pulling him close.

"You poor little motherless darlings," she said.

Then the woman leaned over and reached under her seat. She pulled out a huge basket covered with a red cloth. The smell of fried chicken and potato salad made the children's mouths water.

The woman gave some potato salad to Bailey. She offered a fat chicken leg to the little girl. For a moment the girl watched her brother eat. He nodded to her. She slid off her seat and reached out a chubby hand.

Maya Angelou was the little girl on the train. She was born on April 4, 1928. Marguerite Johnson was the name her parents gave her. To Bailey, she was "my" sister. "My" became "Maya." Soon other close members of the family called her Maya, too. But she was to be Rita or Marguerite to the world outside her home for a long time.

And now the train was taking her to a place that would be home for many years: Stamps, Arkansas. Maya remembers the town of Stamps as a place where she was "greatly hurt and vastly loved." It was a place that would be the strongest influence on her life.

When Maya was a child, Stamps was completely segregated. Segregation in Stamps

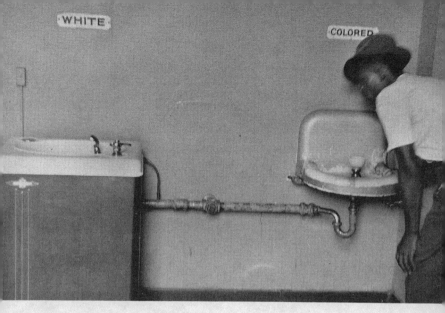

*Because of Jim Crow laws, blacks and whites
had separate drinking fountains.*

meant that it was really two separate towns, a black town and a white town.

Segregation had strict rules called Jim Crow laws. There were separate schools for white children and for black children. Blacks could not drink from the same water fountains as whites. White restaurants wouldn't serve black people. They had to sit in the back of the bus. And they could not vote. These were all Jim Crow laws. Some young black children in towns like Stamps didn't even know what white people looked like! Maya remembers that she didn't believe whites were real people. They were like ghosts. And somehow powerful—to be dreaded.

What kind of person was Annie Henderson, Bailey and Maya's grandmother? Almost everyone called her Sister Henderson. But Bailey and Maya called her Momma. She was tall and straight and strong. She had huge hands. Her hands were so big that just one could cover young Maya's face from ear to ear.

God was very much present in Momma's life. Prayer was a part of everyday living.

This and the following photographs from the TV movie
I Know Why the Caged Bird Sings *show Maya's life in*
Stamps, Arkansas. Bailey was her brother and best friend.

Church was not just for Sunday. The verses
of the Bible and the sermons of the ministers
were part of her.

Momma was loving but strict. She had
two rules: "Always be clean" and "Always
be polite." She did not hesitate to spank the
children if they disobeyed. She fed them and

clothed them. She raised them with love, rules, and a belief in God.

Mrs. Henderson owned the only general store in the black part of town. It sold canned goods, cheese, fruit, and vegetables. It sold everything from shoelaces to balloons. Momma ran it with the help of her second son, Uncle Willie. The family lived in a few rooms behind the store.

The store was an important center for the

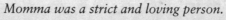

Momma was a strict and loving person.

Maya helps Momma at the store.

black people of Stamps. At the store, they found out who was sick or who had had a baby.

Maya remembers the cotton pickers gathering at dawn in front of the store. Many of them had walked miles to get there. The white farmers came in big trucks to take them out to the cotton fields.

Before the trucks came, the cotton pickers

were hopeful. They often bragged to one another. Bragging was like a game.

"I'm gonna work so fast today, you'll look like you standing still," one would say. And then another would try to make a bigger claim.

But when the pickers came back at sundown, they fell "dirt disappointed" to the ground. Their backs ached from bending all day. Their fingers bled from the sharp bolls that held the tufts of cotton. For all their hard work they made very little money. Momma sold them what they needed. She knew they could never pay back all they owed her.

Maya loved the store. Early in the morning, before it opened, it was a magical place. She loved the smells. The shelves were lined with brightly colored tins. They came from enchanted places. Places she'd never seen. Places like Kansas, Louisiana, and New York City.

Maya and Bailey knew Momma Henderson loved them. But they never understood why they weren't with their mother. Why had she sent them away?

The children began to believe that their mother was dead. It was too awful to think she was happy somewhere without her children.

One day, when Maya was seven years old, their father arrived in a handsome gray car. He pulled up smoothly in front of the store.

Momma ran out.

"Bailey, my baby!" she cried.

"Hot dog, it's our daddy!" cried Bailey, Junior.

Big Bailey was tall and handsome. At first

Maya was happy to see him. He came from California. It was never cold in California. People ate oranges all day. Big Bailey told wonderful stories. Maya loved to hear them. Then one day he told Bailey and Maya to pack. They were moving!

Maya was frightened to leave Momma. Stamps was the only place she could remember. It was home. But Bailey was happy. Happy to be with his father.

On the long drive, Big Bailey said that he was taking them to St. Louis. They were going to live with their mother. Bailey sat up front with his daddy. Maya sat in the back among piles of boxes. She watched the tiny farms and towns go by. And she felt very alone.

3

Betrayal

"Hello, Grandmother Baxter," said Maya and Bailey.

"Hello, children," said an unsmiling woman. Her voice sounded cold.

Grandmother Baxter silently looked the children over from head to toe. Then she lowered her glasses. They were pinned to her dress by a chain.

Without another word to her grandchildren, she turned to Big Bailey. Their father was leaving already. He didn't live with their mother anymore. He sent the children to a corner of the room. They waited to meet their mother.

Maya worried and wondered: *Will Mother like us? What if she doesn't? Will she send us back to Stamps?*

The children heard steps on the porch. Hearts thumping, they looked at each other for a quick moment. The door opened. A woman with butter-colored skin and red lips greeted everyone. She laughed and kissed Grandmother Baxter.

Maya was amazed. Was this her mother? She had never seen a woman as beautiful as Vivian Baxter. Even the white movie stars were not as pretty. Maya reached out to touch her mother's beautiful suit.

Vivian laughed at her shyness. She gave Maya and Bailey, Junior, each a lipstick kiss.

The year was 1935. The country was suffering from hard times. It was against the law to sell whisky. But the hard times did not seem to hurt the Baxters. They lived in a big house in the Negro part of St. Louis. They were a wild and colorful family. They made money from gambling and selling bootleg liquor.

Their mother, Vivian, had four brothers: Ira, Tom, Tutti, and Billy. They were tough and fiercely loyal to each other. They all had good jobs. They worked for the city.

Grandmother Baxter was a very important woman in the black community. Whites respected her as well. St. Louis, Missouri, was in the North, so blacks could vote there. Grandmother Baxter was a precinct captain. She was in charge of seeing that people voted on Election Day. She was rich and powerful.

Maya loved her wild and fun-loving uncles. They weren't afraid of anyone. They were the first powerful black men she had met.

Maya and Bailey lived with Grandmother Baxter for six months. Then they moved in with Vivian and her boyfriend, Mr. Freeman.

Maya felt grateful. She had her own room and nice clothes. But she worried. Would her beautiful mother send her away again?

Maya didn't want to leave her mother and go back to Stamps. But St. Louis didn't feel like home. It was crowded and noisy. She escaped to the library as often as possible. She read adventure stories. She read about beautiful women who lived in faraway places. And about poor people who worked hard and got rich.

The children were often alone with Mr. Freeman because Vivian worked at night. He rarely talked to them. The children did their homework and said their prayers. They were usually in bed when their mother came home. They heard her come in. She'd talk and laugh with Mr. Freeman.

Maya started having bad dreams that made her wake up screaming. To comfort her, Vivian took her into the big bed she shared with Mr. Freeman.

One morning Vivian left for work early. Maya had had another bad dream and was sleeping in her mother's bed. Maya woke up. Mr. Freeman was pressing himself against her. He touched her private places. Maya didn't know what to do. She was just eight years old. Mr. Freeman said he would kill Bailey if she told anyone. Terrified Mr. Freeman would hurt Bailey, Maya kept the secret.

Then a few months later, Mr. Freeman touched her again. This time it was even worse. He hurt her. And again he said he would kill Bailey if she told. Maya loved Bailey more than life itself. She tried to hide her pain, but Vivian discovered the truth. She told Mr. Freeman to leave. Then she took Maya to see a doctor.

What Mr. Freeman did to Maya was against the law. He was arrested. Maya had to go to court and answer questions. Mr. Freeman was found guilty. But he never went to prison. His lawyer arranged to have him released. He was found murdered that very day.

When Maya heard that Mr. Freeman was dead, she stopped speaking. She was terrified. Maya thought his death was her fault. She felt that she was terrible. She thought that if she spoke to other people, they might die, too. Maya would talk only to Bailey. She knew she would never hurt him. She loved him too much.

Bailey and Maya were staying with Grandmother Baxter again. For a while the family gave her special treats. They seemed to understand her pain. After a few weeks the doctor said she was fine. But Maya didn't feel fine. She remained silent.

No one could reach her except Bailey. Her silence made the Baxters angry. They wanted her to play and laugh. Finally Maya and Bailey were put on a train and sent back to Stamps.

At the train station, Bailey couldn't stop crying.

"Mother!" he called. He pressed against the window, hanging on to the sight of his adored Vivian.

Maya didn't care about leaving. She didn't care about anything anymore, not since Mr. Freeman had hurt her. No one understood except Bailey. Now he was miserable, too. She was ruining everything. Little Maya again felt quite lost and alone.

4

The Smell of Vanilla

Maya kept her silence for many, many months. Then, one day, Mrs. Flowers asked if Maya could carry her bags home from the store.

"Go and change your dress," said Momma Henderson. "You going to Sister Flowers's."

Maya gaped at her grandmother. To

Maya, Mrs. Flowers was the most elegant woman in Stamps. Her skin was rich, dark black. She was beautiful and graceful. She spoke softly and wore pretty dresses. Maya ran to pick out a dress.

"Now, don't you look nice," said Mrs. Flowers. She praised Momma's sewing. And then Maya followed Mrs. Flowers home.

Maya couldn't speak, even to please Mrs. Flowers—but that didn't stop Mrs. Flowers from talking to her. Maya loved listening to Mrs. Flowers talk. She especially liked it when Mrs. Flowers pronounced her name, Marguerite. Mrs. Flowers made it sound like music.

Mrs. Flowers's house was cool and dark, just like its owner. The house smelled like vanilla. Even Mrs. Flowers smelled as if she wore vanilla perfume!

Vanilla wafers and cool lemonade appeared on a tray. Mrs. Flowers served Maya as if the young girl were an old friend. Then she took down a copy of Charles Dickens's novel *A Tale of Two Cities*. Maya had read it. But it took on a new power when Mrs. Flowers began reading:

"'It was the best of times, it was the worst of times...'"

The words were like music!

As she closed the book, Mrs. Flowers asked whether Maya liked it.

Maya knew this wonderful woman wanted an answer. She replied even though her mouth was full of vanilla wafers. "Yes Ma'am," she said. These were the first words Maya had spoken to anyone except Bailey in a very long time.

Before Maya left, Mrs. Flowers gave her a

bag of wafers for Bailey. She also gave her some books. One of the books contained poems. Mrs. Flowers asked Maya to memorize a poem and recite it aloud for her on her *next* visit.

Maya ran home to Momma's. One thought repeated itself: *She likes* me! *Me! Marguerite Johnson!*

And after that Maya began to speak again.

Mrs. Flowers had reached out to her—not because she was Annie Henderson's granddaughter, and not because she was Bailey's sister. Mrs. Flowers liked Maya for herself.

Maya visited Mrs. Flowers often. This kind woman helped Maya find her voice. Maya began to delight in reading aloud.

She also began to enjoy spirituals. They were sung with great energy and emotion at church services. Momma sang every Sunday. Maya loved the poetry of the music. The words gave her hope.

Momma Henderson had a strong faith in God and in education. She was not an educated woman, but she was smart. Mrs. Henderson wanted Bailey and Maya to get the schooling she had missed. Education was a ticket out of poverty. One of the biggest events in black Stamps was eighth-grade graduation day.

Maya thought she would burst out of her skin on graduation day. One wonderful thing happened after another.

First, there was the gift from Bailey: a beautiful book of stories and poems by Edgar Allan Poe.

Then, Momma made one of her big Sunday breakfasts, even though it was Friday.

Maya closed her eyes to say grace. She opened them to find a Mickey Mouse watch on her plate.

And finally, there was the beautiful yellow dress. Momma had spent weeks sewing it. When Maya wore it, she felt like a flicker of sunlight.

The ceremony was held at night. As they were leaving, Momma hung a sign on the door. It said proudly: CLOSED FOR GRADUATION.

But something felt wrong on this night. Maya heard it in the principal's voice.

The graduation program had been changed. The principal introduced Mr. Donleavy, a white politician. He was running for reelection.

Mr. Donleavy told them the schools would get better in Stamps. He was giving art supplies and microscopes to the schools—

the white schools, of course. He said the black children would not be forgotten. They would get some new playing fields and equipment for the wood shop and the home economics department.

Maya burned with anger. He meant that whites could become scientists, lawyers, and artists. Blacks could be athletes, maids, and repairmen.

Donleavy hurried away when he was finished. But he left behind a bitter feeling. Now it was Henry Reed's turn to speak. As the top student, Henry was giving a speech. He had memorized it. But part way through his speech, Henry stopped talking. He began to sing:

"Lift every voice and sing
Till earth and heaven ring,
Ring with the harmonies of Liberty…"

It was the song the class had sung all through school. They called it the Negro national anthem. The words were by James Weldon Johnson; the music was by J. Rosamond Johnson—two blacks.

The graduates of 1940 stood proudly then. They brushed aside Mr. Donleavy's cruel message and its meaning for their lives.

5

Sometimes I Feel Like a Motherless Child

Mr. Donleavy's words hurt, but Momma Henderson knew that white people could hurt blacks with more than words. Black people in the South might be beaten or even killed. Momma knew she could not protect the children forever. It was time for them to go back to their mother, Vivian.

Vivian was living in Oakland, California, now. Grandmother Baxter and her sons Tom and Billy lived with her. Momma, Bailey, and Maya took a train to California. Vivian met them in Los Angeles and took her children to Oakland.

But Vivian and the children didn't stay in Oakland long. Several months after they arrived, Vivian married a successful businessman. At last Maya had a real father figure— Daddy Clidell. Daddy Clidell moved his new family to San Francisco. The rest of the Baxters stayed in Oakland.

In San Francisco, Maya went to George Washington High School. It was in a nearby white district. She was one of only three blacks during her first year there.

At George Washington High, Maya had a

wonderful teacher: Miss Kirwin. She treated her teenage students with respect. Maya appreciated that.

"Good day, ladies and gentlemen" was Miss Kirwin's way of greeting the class.

Miss Kirwin did not treat Maya differently because she was black. She didn't feel sorry for her. She didn't hate or ignore Maya. To Miss Kirwin, Maya was simply "Miss Johnson." If Maya gave the right answer, Miss Kirwin said, "Correct." That was what she said to every student who gave a correct answer.

For a while, life was a joy. Maya had Miss Kirwin, Vivian, and Bailey. She went to dance and drama classes in the evening. She dreamed about being a dancer.

But things began to change. Bailey didn't spend much time with Maya anymore. His new friends were tough kids whom Vivian didn't like.

Often Maya came home to hear her mother and Bailey fighting. It wasn't that Bailey didn't love his mother. He loved her very much. Maybe he was still hurt and angry about having been sent away as a child.

After one fight, he packed his clothes in a pillowcase. He gave Maya his collection of books and left. Bailey was only sixteen years old, but he never moved back home again. It was a painful time for Maya.

With Bailey gone, Maya wanted some independence, too. She decided to leave school for a while. She wanted a job on the cable cars. Maya could see herself in a blue uniform. She'd ride up and down the hilly streets of San Francisco. In 1944, more and

*Many women worked as cable car conductors
during World War II.*

more women were working on the cable
cars. They were replacing men who had been
called away to fight in World War II. Maya
was determined to join the work force.

Her mother warned her that she wouldn't
get the job. Colored people weren't hired.

Maya was firm. She was going to do her
best to get that job. Vivian was proud of her
daughter's fighting spirit.

"If that's what you want, then give it everything you got," said her mother.

Maya went to fill out an application. The secretary said, "Come back tomorrow. No one can interview you today."

Maya came back every day. The secretary always said the same thing. Each morning Maya's mother gave her breakfast and money for the cable car. She also gave Maya some words of wisdom.

"Put your whole heart into everything you do," she said. "And pray."

It took four long weeks, but Maya's patience got her the job. She was the first black woman to be a conductor on a San Francisco cable car.

When she went back to school in the spring, she felt different from her classmates. She had money in the bank and new clothes she had paid for herself. She knew what it was like to have a job. And she knew how terrible and wrong racism was. The other students seemed caught up in proms and football games. She didn't know how she fit in.

Maya was very lonely. She got involved with an older boy and became pregnant. She had just turned sixteen years old. She didn't tell her parents until she received her high school diploma.

Vivian and Daddy Clidell stood by her. They wanted Maya to live at home with them. They made sure she got good medical care.

Maya gave birth to a son and named him Clyde. Vivian loved her grandson. She took good care of him and her daughter. But Maya was uncomfortable at her mother's

Maya and a portrait of her son, Clyde.

house. She thought she was making life hard for Vivian and Daddy Clidell. Clyde was barely a year old when Maya moved out with him.

Maya wanted to make her own way in the world. First she got a job as a cook. Then she worked as a waitress. But working and taking care of a young baby was hard, harder than she could handle. Maya was too embarrassed to go back to Vivian, but she didn't know where to turn. She finally went back to the place where she had known love and protection. She went back to Stamps.

Momma Henderson met them at the train station.

"Praise God Almighty, you're home safe," she said. She hugged Maya and the baby in her strong arms. Those arms felt so good and so protective.

The store smelled and looked the way Maya remembered it. With tears in her eyes, she thought, *I'm home*.

Clyde loved Momma from the start. He followed her everywhere. The big woman went about her business with the baby wobbling a step behind. If he fell, she never picked him up. She just paused a moment and waited until he got up by himself.

Maya had forgotten the cruelties of Southern life. One hot summer day, she walked the three miles to the white part of town to pick up a dress pattern. She wore high heels and white gloves. That was how women in San Francisco dressed to go shopping. Maya intended to set an example for Stamps.

When a white saleswoman spoke rudely to her, Maya answered back with an insult. That was a dangerous thing to do in segregated Stamps.

The walk home was long and dusty, but Maya felt proud of herself. She would never forget the surprise on the face of that white woman. She couldn't wait to get home and tell Momma.

Momma was waiting for her on the steps of the store. She looked worried.

Then Momma did something she'd never done before. She slapped Maya across the face again and again. Maya fell down. Momma ordered her to stand up.

Momma told Maya that Arkansas was not California. What she had done was dangerous.

Momma had already packed Maya's and Clyde's things. Stamps wasn't safe for them anymore. Some white people were angry with Maya. If she stayed, they could try to hurt her.

When Maya and Clyde left for the train, Clyde held out his little arms to Momma and cried. Maya looked back. Tears were running down the faces of her grandmother and Uncle Willie.

6

Singin' and Swingin'

In San Francisco, Vivian welcomed Maya and Clyde back. They could stay with her until they got settled.

Maya found a job as a cook at a restaurant called the Chicken Shack. She hated the job, but she loved shopping at a nearby record store, Melrose Records. The woman who owned the store was friendly, even though she was white. There were booths where customers could sit down in private and listen to records. Alone, with her eyes closed, Maya imagined herself singing and dancing. The dream became urgent. Maya wanted to become a professional dancer.

Her first break came from R. L. Poole, a jazz tap dancer from Chicago. Louise Cox, the owner of the record store, had told him about Maya.

Maya was barely nineteen. She didn't know jazz or tap—only ballet. But Poole was struck by her enthusiasm. Maya worked hard to learn all he taught her. She was in heaven. At last, their act, Poole and Rita, opened. But even though they were a success, it was hard to get work as dancers.

Louise Cox liked Maya and gave her a job at the record store. Maya didn't trust

Louise at first. After all, she was white. But, like Maya's old teacher Miss Kirwin, Louise treated everyone equally. A person's skin color didn't matter to her. Louise was one of Maya's first white friends.

At Melrose Records Maya met her first husband, Tosh Angelos. Tosh was a white man who loved jazz as much as Maya did. He was kind to Clyde, and he was a very good husband. Maya was happy at first. She was a full-time mother and wife. She took dance lessons. But her life was still not complete. Tosh did not believe in God. He didn't want Maya to go to church. Maya didn't feel a connection to her roots. When Momma died, that missing link became even more important. Tosh couldn't give Maya what her spirit needed. She divorced him. After the divorce she returned to dancing.

Maya was a professional dancer and singer when she was a teenager.

Maya Angelou in the movie Calypso Heat Wave.

In 1953, Maya began dancing at local clubs and working hard on her routines. People started to notice her. Her dancing was fresh and honest. She had something special that show people call presence. The way she moved and spoke made her stand out from the other dancers and singers.

One night the owners of the very popular Purple Onion nightclub saw Maya's act. So did their singer, Jorie. Jorie invited Maya to a party after work.

At the party Maya sang some calypso songs. Calypso is lively music from the Caribbean islands. Everyone loved it. Jorie was leaving the Purple Onion to go to New York. Maya was asked to take Jorie's job as the singer at the Purple Onion. Maya couldn't believe her good luck. The only singing she had done was in church.

The club managers wanted to give her a new name. "Rita Johnson" wasn't snappy enough. They liked her brother's nickname for her: Maya. When Maya said her married name was Angelos, someone suggested she change it to Angelou. And that's how "Maya Angelou" was born.

With the help of both Jorie's drama coach and the Purple Onion's piano player, Maya developed a routine. She quickly became a favorite. A whole new world opened up to her. She had money, and she had a circle of creative friends: painters, musicians, and writers. Maya began to adapt her poems to calypso music.

She also began to go to musicals and operas. The opera that stole her heart was *Porgy and Bess*. She found out that the company needed dancers for a year-long European tour. She tried out for the part of Ruby and got it. Naturally, she couldn't bring Clyde. Vivian said he could stay with her. Maya was thrilled at the chance to go to Europe, yet she felt guilty. Clyde was too young to be left without his mother. But the opportunity to perform abroad was too good

The program for Porgy and Bess in Israel, 1955.

to pass up. In the end, Maya decided to leave Clyde with Vivian.

Porgy and Bess played in Canada, Italy, France, and Yugoslavia. The crowds loved the black performers. Maya was amazed to find herself in cities whose names she had learned from books and plays.

On a wild bus ride in Italy, from Verona to Milan, Maya wondered if they would arrive in one piece. When the bus finally pulled into the plaza in Milan, a crowd of Italians greeted it. The black Americans, unused to such friendliness from a crowd of white people, stopped talking. For a moment the cast huddled together, not sure what to do. One of the Italians spoke: *"Benvenuti! Benvenuti!* Welcome! Welcome!" The others smiled broadly.

Later that afternoon, Maya explored

Milan on her own. Everywhere she went, Italian people greeted her warmly. Miss Kirwin, Louise Cox, Tosh Angelos, and now the Italians made her begin to think that maybe all white people weren't bad.

Maya missed Clyde all the time. She knew he missed her. All his letters ended with questions: "When are you coming home?" "Can I come visit?"

One day Maya realized she couldn't stand being away from him another minute. She left the company before the tour was complete.

When she rang Vivian's doorbell, everyone came running. Clyde jumped into her lap and would not get down. He looked and looked into her face. The long separation had left its mark. Clyde hung his head when he spoke. His beautiful, smooth skin was now rough and scaly. Clyde was sick. The medicine he needed was his mother's love and attention.

Maya took him out of school for a week. They rode bikes together and went on picnics. Soon Clyde became the beautiful boy Maya remembered.

Instead of shyly hanging his head, he let his thoughts spill out. He told her his ideas. One day he decided to change his name to Guy.

Maya laughed and thought no more of it until she called her son to dinner. Finally she went to his room.

"Why didn't you come when I called?" she asked.

"Because you were calling someone named Clyde. My name is Guy."

He gave her an impish smile. How happy Maya was to be back with him. She didn't care if his name was Guy or Clyde. Any name was fine, now that he was happy again.

7

Years of Activism

Maya found an apartment for her and Guy in San Francisco, near Vivian's place.

Even though she continued to sing, Maya was restless. She knew she would never be a truly great singer. And she also knew that for her, singing was not an important job. The civil rights movement was taking shape. All around the country, blacks were speaking out against segregation. In the South they were marching and boycotting the segregated stores, schools, and buses. Black writers were telling stories of black life.

As a child, Maya had read the works of Edgar Allan Poe, Langston Hughes, and Shakespeare. Mrs. Flowers had shown her the beauty of the spoken word. Maya heard poetry set to music in the powerful Negro spirituals. So it was only natural that she would try using words herself.

She had written poetry since she was a child. With poems she tried to express her feelings of sadness, hurt, and anger. During her singing career she had even written and recorded calypso music for Liberty Records.

Maya knew and admired the works of other black writers. They made her think of writing as something she might do successfully. In fact, she was so impressed that she

Maya was determined to be a writer.

decided to try other forms of writing besides poetry. Maya started to write plays. Then she asked a friend, the writer John Oliver Killens, to read what she'd written.

He told her she had great talent. He urged her to come to New York and join the Harlem Writers Guild. The guild was a group of black writers. They met in each other's homes to read their work to each other. They would give Maya's work the careful criticism it needed to be good enough to publish.

Maya decided to take John's advice. She and Guy moved to New York City.

As a new member of the guild, Maya was allowed to just listen at the first few meetings. But once she became an official member, she had to read her work aloud.

Finally it was her turn to read. The meeting was at John's house. Maya read a play she had written. Her knees shook. The blood pounded so loudly in her ears that she could barely hear her own words. Her play seemed endless.

When she finished, the room was silent. At last one writer spoke up. He pointed out how dull and lifeless her play was. Others chimed in with critical comments. Maya wanted to leave and never come back. She excused herself, but someone stopped her. It was the man who had spoken earlier.

"Maya, talent isn't enough," he said. "You have to work hard at writing."

And Maya began to work harder. She concentrated on writing the way she had concentrated on learning to tap-dance. Meanwhile, she took singing jobs to make money.

The civil rights movement was in full swing in 1957. One night Maya went to hear the

Reverend Martin Luther King, Jr., speak in a Harlem church. A friend, the actor Godfrey Cambridge, was with her. Reverend King was raising money for his organization, the Southern Christian Leadership Conference, or SCLC.

Reverend King spoke of hope and victory. "Embrace the enemy," he said. "But never give up the struggle." He declared that black people would win justice. After he spoke, he led the audience in singing "Oh, Freedom." The words of the old spiritual took on new meaning.

Maya knew that she had to do something to help Dr. King. She and Godfrey Cambridge decided to raise money. They organized a musical revue with black performers. Maya found the perfect name for it—*Cabaret for Freedom.*

Cabaret for Freedom was a success. The

*Dr. Martin Luther King, Jr., was an
important influence on Maya's life.*

performers worked for minimum wage so the
SCLC could make more money. Some even
donated their paychecks, too. After the show
closed, Maya was offered the top job at
SCLC's New York office. Of course, she said

yes. It was an exciting and demanding job. And helping the Reverend Martin Luther King, Jr., was important to Maya.

This was a very exciting time for Maya. She met many new people who had exciting ideas. Among American blacks, there was a new interest in the countries of Africa. They saw Africa as their homeland. Maya's friend John Oliver Killens had some Africans visiting him. He gave a party to introduce them to some members of the American black community.

Maya and Guy were both invited. Guy was now a teenager. He often worked with Maya at the SCLC headquarters. He was very interested in meeting the African visitors.

At John Oliver Killens's party Maya met a South African man named Vusumzi Make.

Vus, as he was called, was very smart and very funny. He liked Maya as soon as he saw her. He liked her so much that he wanted her to come back to Africa with him.

Vus told Maya he admired her strength and good mind. He clearly cared about Guy. And Guy thought Vus was wonderful. Here was a chance for Guy to have a strong African father. Most important, Maya loved Vus. She followed her heart and said yes.

Guy was thrilled. In a few months they were on their way to Cairo, Egypt. They would live in Cairo. Vus was working with black people who had escaped from South Africa. He helped them find homes and jobs.

Cairo was busy, noisy, and strange. Camels and big, new cars shared dirt roads. Vus had a lovely apartment waiting for his new family.

Africa was an exciting place for Maya.

Vus had traditional ideas about men and women. Men worked to make money for their families. Women stayed home with the children to run the house. But Maya never liked being without her own money, and Vus wanted the very best of everything. Then Maya discovered that he had not been paying the bills! Maybe Guy would be forced to leave school. Maybe they would lose their home. Without asking Vus, she took a job. She became a reporter for the *Arab Observer,* an Egyptian newspaper.

Vus was furious, but Maya would not give up her job. Vus knew they needed the money. So Maya stayed at the *Observer.* But things were never quite the same again between them.

They traveled to London and then moved back to New York. Vus was very demanding. He wanted *his* apartment to be fit for a king. He wanted Maya to cook and clean all day. Maya exhausted herself trying to please him.

And then she did something to please herself. In spite of Vus's objections, she took a

SHOWBILL

THE BLACKS

The program for The Blacks *by Jean Genet.*

part in a play. It was *The Blacks,* by a French writer named Jean Genet. She was a star! Everyone praised her.

When the family returned to Africa, Maya and Vus grew further apart. Finally they separated.

Now Maya and Guy were alone again. But this time they were in a foreign country. They were thousands of miles away from home.

8
Mother Africa

Maya wasn't ready to go back to the United States. The year was 1965. She wanted to try to make Africa her home, and Guy wanted to attend the University of Ghana. Ghana was a black country. Its government was run by black people. Maya knew he would get a good education there. He wouldn't be treated differently because he was black.

Maya's friends had helped her get a job

in the country of Liberia. The countries of Ghana and Liberia are both in West Africa. Only one country, Ivory Coast, lies between them. Maya would not be too far from Guy. She planned to stop in Ghana and help him get settled. Then she would go on to Liberia.

Their plane landed in Ghana's capital city, Accra. A group of black Americans who lived in Accra welcomed Maya and Guy. They felt lucky to be in such a friendly place.

Two days after they arrived, Guy went on a picnic with a woman named Ellen, her husband, and some of his other new friends. Maya stayed behind. She wanted to get ready for her trip to Liberia. Guy was late getting back, and Maya began to worry.

Some friends came over to say good-bye

to her. As they were talking, a car pulled up. The front door opened. It was Ellen, and she was covered with blood.

"Where is she? Where is his mother?" Ellen said, sobbing.

A truck had hit their car. Guy was badly hurt. Maya rushed to the hospital. Her son was barely alive. An arm, a leg, and his neck were broken.

Maya could not leave Guy hurt and alone in a strange country. She canceled her job in Liberia. But she had to find work. With the help of a friend from New York, she got a job at the university.

She shared a cottage with two black American women. Fortunately, Guy's injuries were healing well, and he would soon be studying at the university. For a while Maya's life was happy and full.

Maya loved to watch the Ghanaian women. They walked with an easy grace that reminded her of Momma Henderson. And their rhythmic way of speaking reminded her of her uncles. In Ghana, she was surrounded by every shade of brown and black skin—coffee, licorice, caramel, and ebony.

American blacks, with their history of bitter experiences, felt at home in Ghana. Ghana was a prosperous country. Its president, Kwame Nkrumah, was a man much loved by his people. But as much as she loved Africa, Maya knew in her heart that America was her true home.

She was searching in Africa for her history. Who were her people? She longed to find those African roots and claim them as her very own. Sometimes she would rent a car and drive to the countryside. Other times

Maya's African art collection reminds her of her roots.

African friends took her on short trips.

One of the last trips Maya took before returning to America was to a village called

Keta. Strolling through Keta, she met a tall woman. The woman's appearance stopped Maya in her tracks. The woman looked just like Momma Henderson. There were the same beautiful lips and wide forehead. The same broad, graceful gestures. And her voice sounded familiar, even though Maya did not understand the woman's language.

And this woman was sure she knew Maya. Maya's friends explained that Maya was an American. The woman cried and held her head in her hands. Then she took Maya's hand and led her through the market. They stopped at every stall. And at every stall the same thing happened. Each woman vendor gave a cry. Each offered Maya gifts of fruit and vegetables.

Maya was totally confused. By this time she was crying, too. Her friend explained that long ago the whole village had been sold into slavery. Infants were murdered. Mothers and fathers were taken away. The village was burned to the ground. Only a few of the children had escaped.

When these children grew up, they returned. They rebuilt Keta. They never forgot the death of the village. They told the story over and over so that no one would ever forget. The ancestors of the market women were those escaped children. And because Maya looked so much like the people of Keta, Maya's ancestors may have been among the lost mothers and fathers.

Maya was sad and strangely joyful at the same time. She knew about the horrors of slavery. She also knew the great strength of black people, a strength these women proudly shared. She knew she had that strength, too.

Maya Angelou as Kunta Kinte's grandmother in Roots.

She had gotten it from Momma, from Vivian, and from Mrs. Flowers.

Later in her life, Maya acted in a TV

movie called *Roots*. It is the story of a young African boy named Kunta Kinte, who is sold into slavery. When she played young Kunta Kinte's grandmother, Maya may have remembered her experience in Keta.

After visiting Keta, Maya could return to America and blossom. She had found her strong, secure roots growing deep in the heart of Africa.

9

Maya Today

In 1993, Maya Angelou celebrated her sixty-fifth birthday at a huge party given by her friend Oprah Winfrey. Many old friends came to celebrate with her. There is much to celebrate about Maya's life. She has done so many different things.

In 1970, she published the first book about her life, *I Know Why the Caged Bird Sings*. It remains a best-seller year after year.

And she has continued to publish not only books that tell the story of her life, but collections of poems, too. She has written and produced plays and films for TV. She has recorded songs, some of which she wrote herself. She has sung, danced, and acted throughout Europe and America.

She lives in Winston-Salem, North Carolina, where she is a professor of American Studies at Wake Forest University. She has a busy schedule, teaching, writing, and speaking to people around the world. And, of course, she finds time for the special people in her life—her son, her old friends, and her family.

Maya is in great demand as a speaker. She receives thousands of dollars when she gives a speech. Her inaugural poem made her more popular than ever. Her rich voice

Maya loves to spend time with her son.

makes her stories and poems come alive. She speaks slowly and seems to savor each word.

In 1994, Maya received a Grammy. A

Maya speaks to children about racial issues.

Grammy is an award that is given to the year's best singers, songwriters, and musicians. It also honors stories or poems that are read aloud and recorded on tapes and compact disks. Maya won her Grammy for her recording of "On the Pulse of Morning."

She speaks at serious occasions such as graduations or events that honor someone. She seems to find the perfect words to connect her ideas to the people in the audience.

But Maya takes time for fun as well. She recently appeared in a *Sesame Street* special, singing with two little children.

Yet she is a private person. She doesn't like to talk about her family and friends. When she grants interviews, she wants to talk about her work. In her books she often writes about racism. The issue remains important to her. She wants to find ways for black Americans to come together and support each other.

Maya never gave up. She took chances

and was willing to follow her heart. Books have always been a source of joy to her. And three women were very important influences in her life: Momma, Mrs. Flowers, and Maya's mother, Vivian Baxter.

Momma's faith and belief in God gave Maya a sense of right and wrong and of discipline. Momma's house was a loving home.

Mrs. Flowers gave her a love of language and learning. Mrs. Flowers helped Maya believe she was an important and worthy person.

Vivian gave her courage, determination, and a wonderful sense of humor. Vivian also gave her daughter an example of a life lived with style, joy, and laughter.

In a recent interview, Maya was asked what concerns her the most. Maya said she is most concerned about all the young people

Maya and her mother, Vivian Baxter.

growing up without hope. She wants to tell them not to give up, not to stop trying. She said, "You may encounter defeat, but you must not be defeated."

Her own life is an example of that belief. Maya Angelou has never let life defeat her.

Relive history!

Turn the page for more great books . . .

Landmark Books® Grades 6 and Up